Janet Bettesworth is a retired art teacher and stand-up comedian. She has lived in South London for over forty years with two dogs (different ones) and her semi-detached husband.

This is her first novel.

To Oli

Janet Bettesworth

MERCENARIES

AUSTIN MACAULEY PUBLISHERS™

LONDON • CAMBRIDGE • NEW YORK • SHARJAH

A CIP catalogue record for this title is available from the British Library.

ISBN 9781398414617 (Paperback)
ISBN 9781398407220 (ePub e-book)

www.austinmacauley.com

First Published 2022
Austin Macauley Publishers Ltd®
1 Canada Square
Canary Wharf
London
E14 5AA

Acknowledgment

I began this story back to front, with the illustrations. I put up a drawing on Facebook every day, for fifty days, and invited people to invent a back story for each one. I was staggered by everybody's ingenuity, imagination and hilariousness – thanks to all of you:

Leti Bermejo, Peter Stanford, Sarah Fisher, Lesley Duscherer, Margaret McHugh, Neil Ben, Julian Lee, Seanie Ruttledge, Janet Dixon-Hughes, Marilyn Maruako, Toby Vane, Kate Mawby, Mike Potter, Kim Marsh, Tony Moss, Alison Goldie, Julie Wales, Arlene Gorodensky-Greenhouse, Joe George Charman, Annabel Moorsom, Sarah Lynne Ward, Tony Marrese, Judith Liddell-King, Sandra Hale, Sam Dunthorne, Ingunn Lin, Paul Dunn, Cressida Wetton, Mango Stone, Jacquie Hamel, Anushka Tanna, Diane Fitton, Michelle Strutt and Brendan O'Donoghue.

Thank you as well to Maureen Lipman, Elisabeth Luard, Logan Murray, John Fleming, Gillian Garratt and Rowan Low for their encouragement at different times.

The illustrations on the next four pages are examples of the ones that never made it to the book, together with the stories they prompted.

This is **Toto Vargas**. She grew up in a circus family, father an acrobat and mother a glamorous swimmer in a crocodile tank, but she has come to loathe the animal exploitation so goes on loud protest marches and is often involved in sabotage of the many circuses which still cage and whip our furry or otherwise planetary peers. Her least favourite chore involves dust, which, as she often mis-quotes Quentin Crisp: "after the first 3 years doesn't get any thicker" and vacuum cleaners: she has yet to find one that doesn't drive her ears insane.

By Leti Bermejo

Omid Sakari. *An electrician, avid reader and Facebook political commentator (much good that it does him or anyone else). He is a wonderful singer, but only performs in the shower. He recently met a woman in an alley late at night. He was walking one way, she the other. A considerate feminist, he tried to look unthreatening and dropped his gaze, but was surprised to hear her make a low wolf-whistle as she approached. Looking up he saw she was almost a cliche in appearance - blond curls, pure blue eyes and a painted cupid's bow. They both stopped and looked at each other. His heart pounded. She seemed too confident, too bold, almost crazy. Definitely "off". His suspicions were confirmed when she reached up and tweaked him on the nose. "Poor fool," she said in a low voice, blew a raspberry and strode off. He is still thinking about her, wishing he'd asked for her number.*

By Sarah Fisher

Jimbo Hawkins. *He has badly nicotine stained fingers from a life time smoking roll-ups. The love of his life is his flock of racing pigeons, who live on the balcony of his flat, in a large and spotless cage. He has a fondness for gilt edged French furniture, with spindle legs. These he covers carefully with a selection of antimacassars, many of which he has crocheted himself. In his bedroom he has a crimson velvet chaise longue which is rumoured to have belonged to Mandy Rice-Davies.*

By Lesley Duscherer

Paula Martins *is so upset at being chatted up by Dave O'Malley
that she is pretending to use a mobile phone. Both of them know it
is only pretend, and there is a huge waiting game going on as to
who will break first. Spoiler. It will be Dave. Especially if he spots
another unattached woman in the place. She is coping very well with
her anger management, thank you very much. She went through a
Goth phase many years ago, and only ate black food.*

By Peter Stanford

Chapter One

Abstract from "Secrets of the Scissor-Wielding Sisterhood" by Carla Capstick:

A gentle ray of summer sunshine sidled in to explore the recesses of a primrose painted kitchen in Maida Vale. It caressed the spines of a row of books on a humble shelf: it seemed to relish their titles, *The Atkins Diet, Eat Yourself Slim, The Keto Diet Life-Long Weight Loss* and be impressed by the life of discipline and restraint they advised.

A shadow loomed across the sunlit display as Hetty, the owner of the books and the kitchen, lumbered towards the kettle and put out two mugs. The kitchen door burst open, and Jeremy, the plumber, appeared. He sat and waited, watching the bulk of Hetty slithering inside the confines of her gauzy cotton shift.

"How's the diet going, Hetty?" he enquired. "I only ask because—" he pointed at a plate of doughnuts oozing jam in the heat haze and attracting one or two flies.

The thought of flies made him glance down to where his engorged member was urgently pressing against the stiff denim of his work trousers. And the word 'stiff' made matters a lot worse.

If only she wouldn't keep moving about, if only he couldn't hear the gentle suck of her soft flesh sticking and unsticking itself from the dress – if only she had stuck to the Atkins Diet…

"In answer to your question, Jeremy," she murmured, sliding a doughnut into her mouth. "I live for today, and diet for tomorrow…"

His eyes were riveted on her full, jam-smeared lips – a single grain of sugar trembled upon a blonde hair of her downy chin.

With a low groan, he launched himself forward. Too late, the sunshine illuminated the last book on the shelf, *Secrets of the Scissor-Wielding Sisterhood*, and moved slowly down to reveal the enormous shears, with their three-foot blades.

Phew! The first draft is done. I have to write a short performance 'spoken word' piece for my friend Louise's theatre company, Hecate's Spawn. It's five women and a drag queen, and this is for their 2020 show in The Vaults, under Waterloo Station. Just hoping it's #MeToo enough because that's what they're after.

But I'd better introduce myself and let you Google me.

Carla

Chapter Two

It's a tall Victorian house in South London.

Sounds good, doesn't it? But really, it's a medium-height Victorian house in Balham.

On the ground floor lives seventy-six-year-old Alice—the owner and a retired art teacher—and on the first floor, her thirty-nine-year-old lodger Carla, a stand-up comedian. (That's me.)

There is no separate inner door to Carla's flat, a source of some annoyance to Carla.

Carla

Christ, I should never have said yes. Alice asked me down for a cup of tea, dangling the promise of croissants which, fair do's, were OK, not burnt at least, for once. But then she started telling me all about her adventures at the Courtnell Institute Galleries in the '60s, all about 'Sir Aldo' who was the director of the place.

Apparently, Sir Alderney Brunt was also the keeper of the Queen's pictures, so practically royal, until he got unmasked as a Soviet spy and publicly disgraced; it was a massive scandal. She went: "Oh, that was a few years later, but at the time, he was worshipped by everyone! My immediate boss was the curator, Philip Tenchman; he seemed in awe of him as well.

"Then there was this awful woman called Janet Bolt who claimed to be special friends with Sir Aldo because she'd once worked with him at the palace..."

And on, and on...I tried clearing my throat and glancing pointedly at the plate of croissants. "Oh, sorry, do have another one! Well, anyway, one day, I was having a coffee break in the little dingy room downstairs with a large man called Zoltan Wegner, who used to come and photograph the paintings for reproduction.

"Ektachrome, they were called in those days! Big slabs of heavy glass." (No idea what she was talking about.) "Zoltan Wegner always used to bring us cream cakes from Schmidt's in Charlotte Street, so he was very popular!"

"Schmidt's - that takes me back!" she sighed. "It really was like a throwback to a Viennese rococo pastry palace of the 1870s – glittering, tinkling chandeliers, huge, arched mirrors, mounds of glistening profiteroles, scurrying waiters ..."

Blimey, this was making me even hungrier; I grabbed the last croissant.

"Yes, so what happened?" Never known anyone go off on so many tangents, all leading precisely nowhere.

"Oh yes, so where was I? Just sitting there enjoying chocolate cream eclairs with Zoltan Wegner ..."

"And?"

Alice

"Then suddenly in burst Janet Bolt. I could tell her nose was completely out of joint. She said, 'Alice, Sir Aldo and Philip want to see you,' looking very jealous.

"Well, I went upstairs, but all it was, was that a majolica vase from the Flambier-Barry Collection had to be sent off on loan, and they needed me to locate it for them.

"Sir Alderney Brunt was incredibly tall and lanky; he sort of loomed over us in a lofty, aristocratic fashion, addressing a few stiff pleasantries to me as Mr Tenchman knelt on the gallery floor packing the vase with layer after layer of newspaper, then panting slightly as he tied it up in string, with even tighter and more complicated knots.

"I'll always remember the exact words Sir Aldo drawled at that point, as they seemed to be the epitome of *de haut en bas*: N'exagerons pas, Philippe!"

She paused for a second.

"Well, just like you, Carla, I didn't laugh…pretended I didn't understand French!

"The next day Mr Tenchman brought me in some raspberries from his allotment. He lived somewhere like High Wycombe if I remember rightly…"

That job sounds a bit of a cushy number if you ask me, money for old rope.

"What was your salary for that job, if you don't mind me asking?"

"No, not at all, I remember quite clearly; it was thirteen pounds and ten shillings per week."

See what I mean? They say age is just a number, but errrrm—

The doorbell went off at this point. *Thank you, God!*

"Oh, that must be Araminta!" (Her friend.)

"Thanks for the tea, Alice!"

I was out of the door like a shot.

19

Sir Aldo

Alice

Lonely. I was always lonely as an art student in London, back before my gallery job. I remember walking home one winter evening and peering into people's lit windows. They hadn't quite pulled the curtains, and sometimes you got glimpses of family life – someone playing the piano or just disappearing behind a door. There was a sharp tang of coal smoke in the air and clouds rising from chimneys into the winter sky. It was so cold in 1962.

I remember the day I was sacked from my holiday job at the Putney sorting office. My neighbour in the sorting booths was a middle-aged black man who was away sick.

The burly supervisor announced to me, "Old nig-nog's off again. You'll 'ave to sort 'is lot too." Half of the letters were to the same address, and it was quicker to stack these provisionally than to reach over and post each one separately. I pointed this out to the supervisor when he said, "You ain't doing it right!" and continued with my method. Within seconds, I was shown the door. This pattern seemed to prevail in my life, whether in my art classes or these temp jobs. For example, I enraged the German manageress whilst waitressing in Holland Park by not standing with my feet placed together when waiting to be summoned. Maybe, for all I know, I just had a very insubordinate look on my face, all the time.

But anyway, as I was saying, lonely. Later I had no time to feel lonely, all those years as a single mother, having been 'traded in for a younger model'. (I've never understood that phrase, as surely it means that someone would have ended up with me as part of the deal! But they didn't.) When Benjy left home for university and then on to flat-sharing with friends in London, I still had my teaching job.

But now I'm retired, it's all different. When Benjy was in London, it was great to see him, if only fortnightly, but it all changed when Liliana came on the scene.

Liliana with Benjy

It looks like she's the one; they're engaged. She's from a wealthy Italian family with a gorgeous villa in Fiesole looking over Florence, and she's just started a PhD in Feminist and Transgender Studies at Newcastle. Benjy, with his cancer charity job, found it easy to switch to a Newcastle Branch. They both love it there, say it's so much less crowded than

London. You can get everywhere on foot, and you're always bumping into people you know in the street.

I've never been…well, I've never been invited. Last night I had a dream about Liliana spiriting Benjy away – he was a child in the dream. Did I mention Liliana is very beautiful?

Chapter Three

Carla

I'm lugging my Sainsburys carrier bags into the house and smell a delicious aroma of baking, which is most unusual. Then Alice emerges from her living area (kitchen, bedroom, dining room, toilet, shower, all in one room) with a rather woebegone expression.

"Oh, Carla, just wondered – Benjy was coming to stay, but now he can't. Liliana has come down with flu or something. Would you like to help me polish off these scones?"

"Sure, just let me put some of this in the fridge."

When I come back down, I'm with my Yorkshire terriers: Raggy and Blu. It's the one chance they have to explore the back garden, which is normally strictly off-limits. And Alice's Dalmatian adores them.

Every inch of the many shelves in here is covered with knick-knacks; she never throws anything away. Hand-thrown pots, plates, antique teapots, fans, pot plants, a photograph of her father in safari shorts handing Princess Margaret a fly whisk (Alice has a very politically incorrect background), shells, rings, African carvings—all interspersed with

Christmas cards and dangling baubles that she hasn't taken down yet, and it's February!

"That's bad luck to still have them up." I remark.

"Oh, if I really like them, they stay! I'm not a slave to times of the year."

She really has got enough to open some sort of junk shop. On top of all that, the whole place is covered with origami folded paper birds—rows of them!

"What are the origami birds all about? Celebrating something?"

"They're peace cranes. We all used to make them back in the day, in Balham CND. And it's the 40th anniversary of Greenham Common—"

"Er, yes, what was that again?"

"Embrace the Base! The USA at the time was using Greenham Common in Berkshire as a launch base for its nuclear missiles aimed at Russia. So, women decided to set up a permanent protest camp all around the perimeter fence—some of them stayed there for about 20 years!"

"Yes, it vaguely rings a bell; did you go, Alice?"

"Well, there's a bit of a sad story around that. Some friends and I went to spend the night there, in support. I was carrying Benjy in a sling. Had to build a 'bender' tent by slinging a tarpaulin over a branch then securing it down – it was exhausting! Then just as I was getting my breath back, the woman in charge came over to admire the baby and misheard his name as 'Angie'. When I said, 'Oh no, it's Benjy', she looked horrified. 'Oh no, I'm sorry, he can't be here. You're going to have to leave. It's a women's only camp, I'm afraid'."

"Oh wow—unbelievable!"

"Yes, they were pretty radical. Penetrative sex with a man was another thing. It was likened to letting the enemy in over the drawbridge of a besieged garrison – letting down the sisterhood."

I can't think of anything to say—I wasn't expecting a woman—older than my mother was before she died—to suddenly start talking about sex.

"Tea, coffee?"

We sit at her old pine table. There's a copy of The Oldie open at 'I Once Met'.

Classic FM tinkles away in the background. It's quite soothing, as the presenter keeps insisting, but also a bit soporific. Then Julie Walters comes on, extolling Saga Boutique Cruises: "Boutique is small, it's personal—you're never just a number with Boutique." Blimey, old age must make you invisible if you have to pay thousands just to be called by your name!

"I bet you've met some famous people in your time, Alice," I say.

"I have, actually. Once met Lord Snowdon."

I rack my brains. "Oh yes, he was married to Princess Margaret at one time, wasn't he?"

"Oh yes, and he was an incredibly famous photographer."

"How did you meet him?"

"It was just in the street! This was back in the '60s. I was completely broke, and I was going around the arty gift shops trying to sell things I'd made. That's how it was done in those days! This was a very posh shop in Beauchamp Place, and the proprietor had sent me away with a flea in my ear. I was just coming down the steps feeling rejected, and there he was, Lord Snowdon—Antony Armstrong-Jones—as he was

26

before. He said, 'Everything all right?' and I ended up showing him all my art pieces."

"What were they?"

"Oh, they were Christmas cards with tiny little shells stuck on to them in a collage." Of course they were.

"Anyway, he was terribly kind and charming. He ended up saying, 'Well, you can't win 'em all. It's my turn to see Belinda now; what sort of a mood is she in?'"

"Hmm, he sounds really nice," I say.

I don't like to remark that if he was that nice, he could have offered to buy a few cards from her.

"Any other royals you've met?" The scones aren't half bad, actually.

"Oh yes, I met the Queen Mother!"

More mental gymnastics, till I work out that she's Helena Bonham Carter in The King's Speech. But probably older by then.

"It was when I was at the Galleries. She was going to come and have a look at the famous collection of French Impressionist paintings. The whole place was in a panic at the thought of the royal visit, and I'd been tasked with arranging flowers in a huge vase. I was taking tremendous care over the arrangement and thought I was making a really good job of it when this woman called Janet—I've mentioned her before, full of airs and graces, came over and just said, 'Oh no, no, no, that's all wrong!' She grabbed the flowers out of the vase and started all over again, giving me a demonstration *à la Constance Spry* – that won't mean anything to you, but basically, you had to create a perfectly spherical shape, like a round bush, and then have just two or three longer stems poking out. I hated her."

27

"So, how did the royal visit go?"

"Well, that was the thing. We were all lined up in a row while the QM, as we called her, was ushered along by the exalted Sir Alderney Brunt. But she only stopped in front of about every third person. I saw her bypass this Janet woman— and then she came to a halt in front of me!"

"Oooh!" I try to look impressed. "What did you say to her?"

"Well, my mind just went a blank. I ended up stuttering, 'I expect you've got lots of this sort of thing at the Palace?' The stupidest thing I could possibly have said! But she was so kind, she just smiled and said, 'Oh yes, but not quite as nice as this!'"

"Wow," I respond. "And one in the eye for that Janet woman!"

"Indeed." She grins.

Chapter Four

Carla

The thing about London is that it takes an hour by TFL to visit any of my friends who actually live here! I have one local, the afore-mentioned Louise from Hecate's Spawn; she's a great believer in spontaneity, just turning up any hour of the day, claims she gets it from her Balkan ancestors. Also, a vegan, which is quite annoying when she starts going on about it. Luckily, I've been diagnosed with anaemia because, as far as I'm concerned, there's just not enough chicken in the world.

"Hey! Could murder a coffee!" is her opening gambit after an unnecessarily loud rap on my kitchen door nearly makes me drop my phone.

"Hi! Who let you in?"

"Well—obvs! Was your—whatever her name is—downstairs neighbour—landlady."

"Oh, Alice, yeah. Doesn't go out much."

"She seemed to be heading for the bins. She looks a right tart!"

"She is."

"Why does she need that much slap on her face just to put the rubbish out?"

"Well, you know, she's from the '60s. They can't go out of doors without a full face of makeup."

"To be fair, it's pretty much the same nowadays." (She always has to correct me.)

"Hmmm."

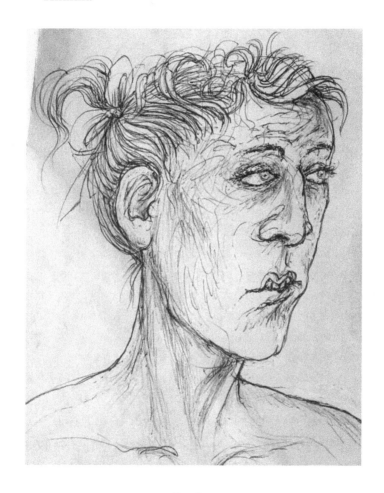

Louise

"What's it like, living with her downstairs?"

"Hideous! You can hear every footstep. Every clumping footstep. Non-stop sneezing and farting."

"What, really?"

"Yep, you can hear her trudging to the toilet. Then it's like the trombone section tuning up."

"Or cannons going off on Remembrance Day?"

"You always have to trump me, don't you, Louise?" (She doesn't laugh.)

"Oh, I can see why you're a comedian. Yes, I'd love a coffee; thanks so much for asking."

Talking about my lodger status with Louise always makes me feel a little sour, as she has somehow managed to blag herself a self-contained flat in a beautiful almshouse on Wandsworth Road.

"Any more tales to tell about the old bag?"

"No, not really. Well, it seems like she's pissed off the black community around here."

"No! Do tell!"

"She goes to urban hairdressers to save money. Apparently, they charge about half anywhere else. Anyway, they have Christian Radio on the whole time, and they were interviewing a sportsman. He said, 'God made me a Christian. But he also made me fast. When I'm running, I feel His pleasure'. So, of course, dear Alice bursts out, 'What a load of baloney! So, when I'm hobbling, I feel His displeasure, I suppose!'"

"So, how did the hairdressers react?"

"They just went very quiet. Been having a good time up till then, I expect! Suited Alice though, she said she could do her crossword in peace."

"Wow, just wow. Old people, they get away with it though, don't they, every time?"

Alice

"Pitter patter, pitter patter, let it pour. Clitter clatter, clitter clatter, let it roar. The-ese are the pretty little April showers," came suddenly into my head, hearing the rain on the roof. This was the first piano piece I was taught at Kitale School in Kenya when I was seven years old. The more I think about it, the more I realise that I must have been bullied consistently all the time I was there, giving myself away as a potential victim the very first morning in September 1951. Sitting at the long breakfast tables, a boiled egg in front of each child, I realised with terror that I had no spoon to eat mine with and not enough courage to ask for one. I just sat there miserably, my chin starting to wobble as I fought the tears. An older boy opposite noticed and got me a spoon. This was the only act of kindness I can remember. Later that morning in the classroom, we were told to get changed for games, and I had no idea how to do this. In a haze of misery, I heard the teacher shout 'Alice!' and found I had pulled down my knickers by mistake, and all the children were staring and giggling.

The girls were the worst, and the large white African contingent from South Africa was far more hard-boiled than I ever was and much more socially integrated, as I'd been home-schooled up until then. In the dormitory, they zeroed in on my mother's delicious home-made fudge she'd packed in my little red attaché case and told me I had to refill it at half-term for them, or I'd be sorry. Any kind of sweets was the equivalent of crack cocaine at that school. We must have constantly been hungry because I remember children eating the resin from gum trees and sometimes toothpaste.

The time of day I looked forward to the most was 'Rest': two hours after lunch on our beds in the dormitory when it was possible to cry quietly on my own with nobody knowing—or on better days read Enid Blyton's 'Malory Towers' about a happier boarding school. I was given an official title, 'The Wet', and the other kids would chant "Wet sap! Jerry Jap!" as I walked past. Being born with a squint didn't help. My parents had had it operated on when I was three, but as the Nairobi hospitals in 1947 weren't that advanced, I'd ended up with a much more pronounced one.

My most vivid memory is of a ritual beating I was given in the dorm. There was a reason I was given this punishment, but I can't remember it. I was made to strip naked and stand by the end of my bed. The girls queued up, and each one gave me a single whack with her hairbrush. It might have been for 'being a cry-baby'. Children were copying the adults: corporal punishment was standard in all the Kenya schools, known as 'being given the takje' (hit with a plimsoll). Some of the children may have seen their fathers beating African farm labourers with a *kiboko*, a hippo hide whip.

My piano lessons stopped because two other little piano students told me, "Miss Simpson says she wants to whip you," and somehow, I never went to another lesson.

No one ever seemed to complain about the way things were in those days. If you were unpopular and unhappy, you felt a sense of shame and assumed it was all your own fault. Years later, my cousin's husband told me that during his time at the same school a few years earlier, the other boys had tied him to the bedsprings of his bed, upended it against the wall, and left him there.

It now seems so long ago that remembering it gives me no pain, just a kind of wondering disbelief. And I hardly ever think about it unless something like the old 'Pitter patter' song jumps into my head at the sound of the rain: the somehow furtive crepitation on the glass roof of the extension. As if the rain is saying, "Yes, I know I've rained continuously for the whole of February, flooded huge parts of the country, and made people lose their homes, but I just had to take another pee, hope you don't mind." And it helps me fall asleep.

Usually, I'm woken by a train or my bladder. I am very far from being able to say, "That's the 5.57 from Brighton." But every morning at about that time, the first train—the one I call the 'train d'urgence' (I'm a bit of a Francophile)—slices through the silence like a knife, all on one note.

Then they start speaking to me: "Novosibirsk, Novosibirsk," a slow clanking sound like my limbs when I get out of bed in the morning. 'Novosibirsk' sometimes identifies as 'Uttar Pradesh' or 'Blood of the Lamb' and sometimes speeds up remarkably, though the rhythm's the same.

I really love my train messages. Well, I have been here for over forty years.

I don't know where 'Blood of the Lamb' comes from; I used to be a church-goer for a time when Benjy was young and went to Sunday School at the Church of England St Mary's Church in Balham High Road. They were going to have an ecumenical evening, and I volunteered to host it. As an art teacher, I had lots of paintings up on the wall, and before the meeting, I stopped in front of one of them.

It's by a friend of mine, Leti Bermejo: a wonderful canvas of a naked couple intertwined in a post-coital embrace while in the foreground sits an enormous striped cat just staring past their heads towards a light-filled window. I wondered if perhaps I should take it down but then thought, *No, that would be me pretending to be something I'm not.*

When the guests arrived—a mélange of Methodists, Baptists, Catholics and Pentecostals—I offered them tea and biscuits, and then as I was leaning against the mantelpiece, a Methodist lady (who'd arrived late and didn't realise I was the host) sidled up to me and said, *sotto voce*: "Who on earth would have a painting like that up on the wall?"

I said, "Goodness, yes, ooh, I see what you mean." So much for not pretending not to be me. The thought came: *Before the cock crows three times, ye shall betray me.*

Chapter Five

Carla

Got a paid gig tonight, £50. Perhaps it's a bit 'audacious' as my comedian friend AKB would say, to be trying out new material: a mash-up between assertiveness issues and my dead mum—oh dear, it doesn't sound very promising, laugh-wise, what was I thinking? Fifty quid is about the most I ever get, apart from the odd freak appearance at a Rugby Club in Tonbridge or wherever.

Louise has announced that she's thinking of trying stand-up. "Keep the old juices flowing." I think she hasn't aced many auditions recently so she's coming tonight and we're driving from here. We're even thinking we might eventually do an Edinburgh show together.

She bursts in, larger than life, as usual, kiss on both cheeks and one for luck.

"I saw your old biddy by the bins again! The garbage was strewn all over the front garden!"

"Oh, it might have been a fox or something—did you offer to help?"

"Are you nuts? No, not getting involved. She seemed frantic!"

"I think she may be pissed half the time. Did you notice her recycling sack? It's mostly Schweppes Tonic bottles. Partial to a G&T."

"Poor old cow. But your rent's a steal, though, right?"

"Only cos she hasn't cottoned on to the going rate. She doesn't know if it's tomorrow or Christmas. She's as stingy as fuck otherwise."

"How do you mean?"

"Oh, god, I wouldn't know where to begin. She doesn't let my dogs go in the back garden for a start. That would make a hell of a difference to my life, I can tell you. And to Raggy and Blu."

My two adorable Yorkies look up, and Raggy gives a little yap. "Yes, Deidre the naughty Dalmatian's got it all to herself, hasn't she, Raggy? Dat's so, so not fair!" (I should stop addressing the dogs in baby talk, it's so not cool.)

"Yes, and Deidre would like it too; they love it when they pass each other in the hall. Like ships in the night! Mind you; some strange things have been known to happen in that garden. I get a direct view out of this window."

"Oh, like what?"

"Well, this is so weird. You know she has her toilet and shower at the end of that big room where she basically sleeps, eats, and lives her whole life?"

"What's that room like, by the way?"

"Oh, it's a shambles, of course. Quite big, though, that's the saving grace. And you should see the Airbnb—it's really nice. A Nigerian guy called Richard set it up for her, ensuite, the works, it must be a nice little money-spinner. Whereas her own space—I have to say some of her habits are worrying. For example, when she had the extension done, she had this big dog-flap hole built-in, so the room barely gets warm enough with all the radiators on."

"I know, I can guess—she sticks the gas ring on!"

"Exactly! Massive fire waiting to happen! I've noticed that the tray she has near the cooker is singed all around the edge. So, it's not just me being paranoid."

"Oh blimey, I hope you've got some accident insurance in place."

"Oh well, fingers crossed—that guy Richard made her put some smoke alarms up."

"Well, good, wouldn't want you going up in smoke— have you finished Part Two of the piece for Hecate's Spawn?"

"Indeed, I have. I'm calling it 'Harvey Weinstein: The Day Before #MeToo'."

"Let's hear it then!"

"Harvey Weinstein: The Day Before #MeToo.

Dear Diary,

My life is one long endurance test, like Job out of the Bible—one fucking catastrophe after the other. The pool guy never turned up to fix the pleasure pump, that was Tuesday. I said he could keep his job if he sent his little sister Juanita along, but—never happened—where's reliability gone? He's fired, obviously, but the rota up on the kitchen wall has fallen down again. That rota is at the root of my whole karma and being. I'm a man, after all, an Alpha male. I need Bernice arriving in my bedroom at 8 am on the dot, followed at half-hourly intervals by Candy, Renata, Susie, Suzette, Angie, LaBelle, Joyeuse, Minnie, Julia, Marilyn, April, Roberta, Eloise, Sandra, Valerie and Bubbles. Some guys are amazed by my appetite and stamina, but they are not real guys, not real men. These women cater to my needs, and they're happy to do so. They know that they are playing a vital part in keeping me, the ruler of an empire, happy. They fight each other sometimes for mouthfuls of me—I'm a god after all, and I've heard them talk about its magic properties. What an opportunity I'm giving to each and every one of them.

But, as I say, the damn rota has gone missing off the wall, so I'm opening up more slots for any random starlets or actresses who fancy their chances. It's a fucking pain cos, to be honest, they're less obedient.

And them having their eye on what they can get out of me is frankly a big turn-off."

"I like it!" says Louise. "Just Part three to do now. Where do you get your ideas from?"

"Well, that one came from Alice, believe it or not. She was reminiscing away—"

"As is her wont!"

"And she said she had a fleeting encounter with the CEO of Playboy UK, Victor Lownes, back in the '60s. He tried to hit on her at a party. And later she saw his state-of-the-art kitchen in Montpelier Square, and it had a rota just like that, pinned up on the wall."

"Unbelievable."

"And it seems that all the female staff there were up for it – got lavish gifts."

"Well, don't let's go down that route for the thing you're writing. What about this weird thing you were going to tell me about Alice's toilet, though?"

"Oh, yes. Well, I was noticing single pieces of toilet paper issuing forth from her toilet window and floating off into the breeze. This was last summer. I was thinking, oh my god, has she finally flipped? Are they going to have to cart her off to a home? Cos that wouldn't suit me at all…"

"Sounds revolting. Did you find out what was happening?"

"Yes, I came straight out with it and asked her, said 'By the way, could you tell me what all those white squares of paper are, all over the patio? She says, 'Oh, it's when I rescue ants and spiders and flies from the basin or crawling up the window. It's easiest to just coax them on to a bit of loo paper and then quickly throw it out of the window – they just float away on their own private parachute and land who knows where? Up to the gods!' I said, 'Are you a Buddhist, Alice?' She says, 'No, just can't bear to end the life of an innocent creature!'"

"Nam Myoho Renge Kyo! Nam Myoho Renge Kyo!" Louise begins chanting.

"Hmm, where did you learn that?"

"Oh, it was in a play I was in. Or perhaps in a theatre workshop? Maybe the one where I met you? It's great, isn't it? Nam Myoho Renge Kyo! You have to say it over and over. Good for the nerves, by the way!"

Louise collects chants. Now I know I'm going to hear that on repeat all the way to the gig. Really annoying, and it makes me way more nervous, not less.

Chapter Six

Alice

Just having a think today—about myself! Not something I often do. I was wondering—*am I fundamentally dishonest?*

I've pretty much not stolen or shoplifted anything for the past fifty years, but I still stuff those sugar sachets into my pockets in a café—comes in handy for my Airbnb. Even more shameful—my doctor's surgery has marvellous thick paper towels—really useful for the dog. In the rare gaps between dogs during the last fifty years, I've noticed how extraordinarily (almost uncomfortably) clean everything is!

From 1970 to 1971, I shoplifted every single day. It must have been a cry for help, as they say. It was like giving a present to myself, but I got a real thrill out of it too. Clothes from all the big stores, including a fur coat from Harrods! I remember the incident that stopped me in my tracks so that I've more or less never done it again.

It was in the rather decadent '20s' revival dimly lit Biba's basement. Tiffany lamps softly illuminating racks of silky palazzo pants and knickerbockers to the strains of 'A Whiter Shade of Pale'. I was wearing a long black coat from somewhere else and had my black spaniel, Fred, on the end of a length of a string. My usual technique was to have a shawl casually folded over my arm, to absently drape several items from the shop over it as if I was planning to try them on. Then I'd change my mind and virtuously replace them—except that one had somehow got hidden under the shawl.

I never speeded up – everything was very lethargic as I ambled out into the street.

Davina

Dawn

Except for this time—I was confronted by a huge man in uniform with a whistle on a cord. No use trying to do anything after his 'We have reason to believe', but be shepherded back into Biba's and led downstairs into an office. There was a sort of androgynously glamorous woman, called Davina— complete with a cigarette in a cigarette holder—waited with

Dawn—the young female store detective who'd spotted me—who was got up cleverly like the typical 'dolly-bird'.

Davina glanced at me with bored contempt and got on the phone to the police.

She told Dawn to stand guard outside the toilet when I asked to go. Maybe I'd been hoping to melt back into the crowds, but very quickly, I was in a black saloon with opaque windows on my way to having my fingerprints taken at South Kensington Police Station. How different everything was then! After a long, miserable wait, I had to be interviewed and make a statement, sitting opposite a large middle-aged police officer. I'd been in my first art teaching job for just a year, at a boys' school in Walthamstow, and what I urgently needed to know was, would my employers be told? The policeman had, I remember, a large thick tome on the desk in front of him, and in answer to my question, he started riffling through the pages.

"Now, let's see, chapter 15, sub-section 27," he said as he ran his finger down the page.

"No, not there, it's bye-law No. 8, hold on." Till finally: "Ah, there it is! No! We will not need to inform your employers."

I can only believe this was an extraordinary act of kindness. A teacher friend of mine had not only been sacked but also permanently blacklisted for giving one marijuana joint to a friend, who shopped him on being raided by the police. All I had to do was attend court the following week and pay a £200 fine.

How different my life would be now—I live on my job pension, which I have to say is not really enough to keep me going, well, not nearly enough if I'm honest, what with the mortgage, which seems to get bigger year on year. I'm sure the idea was that it was meant to get smaller! The rent from upstairs and the Airbnb just about keep me afloat.

Carla

We're at the gig, and I'm just about to go on. If you're wondering what it's like, it's absolutely the worst; I'm thinking, *why on earth do I do this* – so terrified (well, it's sometimes better if there's a toilet within reach and I can have a shit, but there isn't). No one would think I've done over 300 gigs.

This venue is actually directly underneath London Bridge and was really hard to find the first time I went there. Google Street View just threw its hands into the air and gave up when it had to go under the bridge; in other words, all the perspective lines juddered into a surreal collision. Had to end up picking my way down vertiginous stone stairs that reeked of piss.

This time I came by car. My hypothesis is if the Street View drones can't see under London Bridge, neither can the traffic wardens, so that's where I park. Plus, it's Alice's old Morris Traveller, complete with a 'Disabled' badge, so that covers a multitude of sins. She lets me borrow the old rust-bucket sometimes to get to gigs if they're not too far. I love it because I get instant props from the other comedians who think it's incredibly cool. Louise quite likes riding in it too. I

Jeb Couch

do a comedy bit sometimes:

"This old guy actually flags me down; then he's like 'Wind the window down!' Then he says, ''Ow much, love?'

'Oooh! Well, I'm very flattered, but I'm not really that sort of girl'.

'Not you, love! The motor! The Morris! The Moggy'!"

Now, I'm going to be on any second – don't these MCs realise what torture this is? I'm taking deep breaths to fill my lungs to bursting point and slowly exhaling while the guy seemingly performs his entire forthcoming Edinburgh show—that's not what MCing's supposed to be about. He's already drenched my left trouser leg before the break in a comedy raffle of a bottle of wine – whoever won it can whistle for it because Jeb (Jeb Couch) decided to yank the cap off and spray the audience. I was really scared that the dodgy looking lamp was going to tumble into the alcohol on the floor—because there's no fire exit here in any shape or form whatsoever.

My phone's just gone off, earning me a dirty look from Jeb—he's got some nerve, after all his shenanigans. I slip out the door to answer it, and it's only Alice, saying it's an emergency, she needs the car and I have to come home!

"What emergency?"

"I have an Airbnb guest from South Korea who speaks no English, and she's lost somewhere; we know not where!"

"That's not an emergency, Alice, as you well know—got to go—please never ring me at a gig again!"

Alice

One of my Airbnb guests, a lady called Dong Seeon from South Korea, has gone missing! She had messaged that she would be very late checking in, as she hadn't realised that Korea was GMT+9. I replied with the times of every train from Heathrow, together with a sketch-map of the walk from Balham Station to here.

At 1:30 am, she rings, and I can just about understand her trying to say that she's near. I go into the lamp-lit, frosty deserted street and walk up and down; is that a figure? No, just a lamp post. I ring Carla to try and get my car back in case it's needed. No dice—she's quite rude. Back inside, another phone call: "I am in Taireeploce." Really hard to understand, so I ask her to spell it: it comes out 'CEARCEETLOSE'.

We're getting nowhere, but she suddenly spots a man putting out the rubbish.

"I ask him."

I hear their conversation going around and around, so I say, "Let me speak to him," and he explains.

"This is Pearce Close in Mitcham. Let me go inside and put on my glasses so I can order her a cab; it's freezing out here."

"Thank you so much," I say. "What's your name?"

"Samuel. It's nothing. Everybody needs somebody."

She's starting a course tomorrow at an end-of-life care home for Jewish dementia sufferers in Battersea. On its website, which I'm perusing for something to do, it says they've installed an old Morris Minor in the garden for a man who's obsessed with them and kitted out an office for a woman who misses hers! Gosh, it sounds like it would be worth converting to Judaism!

About twenty minutes later, there's a commotion at the door—she's arrived! The first thing she asks is, "Can I smoke in the room?"

No-o-o-o-o-o!

Carla

I rush back into the venue; Jeb is eye-rolling at me like he's had to do far longer than he wanted. He announces me without much of a fanfare, and I give him the usual perfunctory handshake. As soon as I slide the mic out of its holster and speak: "Hell-o-o-o! Let's just get one thing out the way, right? I'm 39, and I've still got a pulse!" (This in reference to the fact that the average age of the other comics is 23)—I'm fine.

"No, it's a proper clinical diagnosis – it's an acronym, it stands for Perpetually Unfeasibly Low Self Esteem. My friend Louise says, 'Basically it means you're unfit for purpose; you're a car that's failed its MOT, you're a book that's been remaindered, you're the last thing left on the table at a fire-damage sale—a bootleg copy of Love Story in VHS…or a home enema kit, one careful user…'"

(Audiences love a bit of self-deprecation.) "I said, 'That's a bit harsh, Louise!' She said, 'Well, what about when your mum died?'

"She's talking about the undertakers: all the coffins were stashed on shelves with the cheaper ones at the bottom, then it went up and up, the Superior, the Prestige, the Supreme, and then, the Ultimate! The Funeral Director lady introduced them to me: 'If I may offer a word of advice, I always recommend the ultimate for looks and durability, plus it's got an interior triple sprung mattress for comfort'.

"I looked at this thing, she winched it down, it looked like a massive toffee that had been sucked all over by a giant and then spat out; it was all glistening. I said, 'What actually happens to this coffin?'

"She looked at me as if I was a bit simple, and said 'Well, your mother is being cremated, isn't she?'

"I said, 'What about that one?' (Bottom shelf, very plain.)

"She said (quavering voice), 'Don't do something you're going to regret for the rest of your life! You can't put a price on a mother's love, can you?' I could see a perfect tear trembling on her eyelid.

"She said, 'I'm afraid that is what we call the Pauper's Coffin'.

"Then there was an uncomfortable silence; you could have heard a pin drop. It felt like the whole village where my mother had lived was listening in. So, I said, 'Yes, yes, I'll take the Ultimate'.

"£4,778.63! Of course, afterwards, I was bankrupt! I started to have heart palpitations and irritable bowel syndrome and started to feel a bit lonely – the doctor said I should try to get more involved in the community, so here I am!"

Then comes the bit about finding a life-coach called Sheena, then I end with the audience chanting: "NO! You can stuff my mum's ashes up yer bum! I don't wannem! Do you hear?

"Ner-ner-ner-ner-ner, NO!"

You had to be there.

Chapter Seven

Alice

Bombshell! Having just said goodbye to Dong Seeon that morning (she gave me a lovely little Korean handkerchief sachet: 'is a gift'), I welcomed in my latest Airbnb guest, Linda, from East Kent, quite a smartly dressed, slim woman who seemed a little nervy but quite pleasant. She said, "Oh, it looks very nice. I'm an Airbnb Super-Host myself, you know."

I said, "Oh, perhaps we could compare notes at some point?" I was just being friendly, but that got no response. I pointed out all the things in the usual way, the ensuite, the mini-fridge, the Wi-Fi password, etc., and said, "Well, I'll leave you to it. I'll be around if you need anything."

I'm watching The Voice, as it's a Saturday, when there's a knock on the door and there she is, all dressed up in her coat, with her luggage all around her! She has retreated to the end of the passage for some reason, as though keeping her distance, and says, "Didn't you get my text message?"

"No, sorry, I was watching telly. Is everything all right?"

"No, it certainly is not. It's the trains! I wasn't expecting this! They're every two minutes! It's unbearable! Literally every two minutes, I timed them! How can I possibly sleep with that going on?"

My heart absolutely sinks at this. "Oh dear, is there maybe something we could do?"

"No! No! It's just not up to my standards. The milk's out of date; the bread's out of date—"

Linda

Further sinking feelings.

I say, "No, they're quite fresh! They were frozen the day they were bought, a week ago, and defrosted today!"

"Yes, I see what you mean only too clearly. There are standards, and there are standards, but it's simply not up to my standards. And by the way, I recorded the train noises on my phone as proof. Obviously, I've also cancelled the other two stays I had booked with you later in the month. I'll have to find a hotel; it's most inconvenient. Goodbye!" she says in a very hostile, frosty manner.

Well, I have a strange feeling of having been physically beaten up. And I just can't stand that expression 'up to my standards', at the best of times. There's a huge sense of unfairness.

Carla

We're sitting in Louise's exquisite almshouse. The invitation was ostensibly so I could show her Part Three of the #MeToo piece for her troupe, but I think she really just wants to rub my nose in how she's ended up in this gorgeous place. At the housing interview, she played the 'indigent actress' card, the distressed gentlefolk vibe – no idea how she pulled it off, at the age of 37! Perhaps they were just dying for new blood and a fresh young face; well, I don't blame them really, and she's been pro-active in getting the damp seen to, so the other residents adore her.

We're drinking truly disgusting Green Matcha Tea.

"How are things back at Alice Towers?" enquires Louise.

"She's looking a bit down in the mouth. I heard her having a bit of a barney with one of the Airbnb guests, no idea what was going on."

Araminta

"Hasn't she got any friends?"
"Oh, yes, one or two. The main one is called Araminta."
"Blimey."

"Yes, you should see them together. They just need one more, and you'd have the witches from Macbeth!"

"Oops! Unlucky! I didn't hear that. Where's Araminta from?"

"Well, she lives in the next street, but I think she comes from somewhere in Kent originally, she always says, 'We was.'"

"Oh yes," says Louise, "that means she's certainly from Kent. Probably East Kent, I'd say."

Ever since drama school, Louise has fancied herself as a dialect expert.

"Now, I can't wait to hear Part Three," she says.

"Sure, want me to read it out?"

"No, I'll do it; it'll get me into practice for the performance."

"You might be a bit surprised by the content."

"Let's wait and see, shall we? Here goes:

"Who is History's Greatest Monster? Definitely got to be a man, hasn't it? Or… I'm going to try and level the playing field: this one woman was so evil that I should probably apologise on her behalf in advance—unless she's been misjudged? She did hang 650 people upside down and let their blood drain into buckets for her supper.

"And her bath. As part of her skin-care regime. Anyone?

"Yes, Countess Elisabeth Bathory from sixteenth-century Transylvania! Now, we all have our hobbies, don't we? Hers just happened to be lace-making and sadism. Are you sitting comfortably? Then I'll begin. It all started in her massive ancient creaking Gothic castle, Chaxteetsay, high up on a hill—and a small flyer came through the door.

"'Hello, we are Monika and Magda; we are cleaning service for you. We are careful, and conscientiously, you can hire us of two hours or more, smiley emoji'.

"When she saw this, the Countess was seen rubbing her hands together and muttering: 'Two for the price of one'. A week later, Monika and Magda were reported not to have dusted the top of the armoire properly. So, Monika was stripped naked, coated with honey and tied up in the garden to be eaten alive by crows and small rodents, and Magda was sewn up alive inside the belly of a dead ox.

"How are we to interpret this? You might think it was a bit harsh, but my friend Agnes, professor of Comparative History at the University of the Third Eye, said, 'Standards were different in those days! Nowadays, you'd just leave a note on the fridge, passively aggressively suggesting they might like to do a bit of dusting—it's exactly the same!'

"I said, 'Thank you, Agnes,' but Agnes wouldn't shut up.

"She said, 'It's just like this #MeToo witch-hunt! In the 1970s, it was completely normal to sexually harass young girls and boys as much as humanly possible. They'd feel insulted if you didn't. "What, you ain't been felt up today? – MINGER!" Children were offered up on silver platters to be feasted on by paedophiles. In short, it was an honour to be groped by an elderly gentleman in a tracksuit!'

"Anyway, Elisabeth had a get-out-of-jail-free card, as her cousin was the prime minister, and if that didn't work, she always carried around with her a dried-up afterbirth which had inscribed on it: 'When in danger, you may call on the spirits of 99 black cats to rescue you'.

"Elisabeth was a bit cat-like herself, with jet black hair and very pale skin. She spent hours on end staring at herself in the mirror, a bit like the Queen in Snow White, except not so benevolent. Her housekeeper, Erzie, was an outstandingly ugly old crone. I'm allowed to say that cos there was no PC in those days. Nowadays, she'd be called a Real Woman. She worshipped her mistress, and Elisabeth liked her because she always looked good standing next to her. Anyway, one day when the Countess was about 50, she noticed that her skin treatment of arsenic and lead wasn't working so well anymore: 'I seenk I am losing my looks!'

"So that's when Erzie suggested, 'Mistress, why you not try bathing in the blood of virgins. Because you're worth it!' They started on a modest scale, but just like L'Oréal, or Laboratoires Garnier, they had to keep researching and refining, and soon the Countess had got through around 400 of the local village girls—purely in the interests of science.

"The police issued a statement: 'There is nothing to link the Countess with these disappearances. Eighty-five percent of the village girls have gone missing. Eighty-five percent of the village girls have gone to work for the Countess. It remains a complete mystery'.

"It was all shaping up to be a happy-ever-after story. But sadly, about two years later, the Countess was again screaming at her mirror: 'Oh. My. God. My skin is showing ze tell-tale signs of ageing! What am I to do?'

"So Erzie, with her out-of-the-box thinking again, suggested: 'Mistress, why you not pretend to set up a finishing school for ze daughters of ze nobility? Zeir blood is so much finer, so much purer, than zeez chavs! Blue blood, veez added whor-har-haar!'

"Well, that's just where it all went wrong. When the first batch of posh girls went missing, there was a massive hue and cry, the castle was invaded, and all the household, including Erzie, was arrested and tortured to death. But not the Countess—aristocratic immunity.

"But she did get walled up inside one room of her castle and had to have her food posted through a slit in the wall. That's when pancakes were invented. Three years later, she was found face down on the floor dead, with a note by her side which said: 'Just so you know, I have called upon the spirits of 99 black cats, to tear out the hearts of my judges'.

"Well, all I can say is, it wasn't her fault that Botox and fillers hadn't yet been invented. And I'm not prepared to judge her—I'm scared enough of black cats as it is—thank you very much!"

"What do you think? Do you like it?" I ask eagerly.

"Not sure. I mean, it doesn't exactly chime with the #MeToo mission statement."

"Does it have to, though? I just thought, why should men have the monopoly on being bad? Why can't we have some fun too? Otherwise, we're just over-sanitising women, aren't we? Claiming to be above reproach – sugar and spice and all things nice, a hundred per cent of the time!"

"I suppose," she says reluctantly.

Chapter Eight

Carla

Tonight, I get a phone call—oh god, it's her downstairs.

"Have you got a gig tonight?"

"No-o-o—" (cautiously.)

"Oh, good, because I've got something I want to discuss with you."

"Err—" (I'm about to say it is possible I'd be busy for other reasons.)

"I'd like to offer you a paid job."

My ears prick up at this. "Oh, yes, what?"

"Well, you'd need to come down and have a chat about it. Bring Louise if you can."

"Louise?"

"Yes, I can't explain any more now. Come at seven, and I'll do some beans on toast or something."

She really likes to push the boat out.

Not really looking forward to this!

Later. OMFG. I thought my life could get weird but didn't think it would happen through the medium of my ancient landlady. When Louise and I go down there, she's got four chairs in a sort of circle, and her pal Araminta (older if anything) is sitting on one of them, with a mug of tea.

Meanwhile, Alice is tussling with her Vax vacuum cleaner while sitting in a moth-eaten wing chair.

"I'm going to have to put a higher age limit on my guests," she declares, viciously snapping at the spindle with a pair of scissors. "These younger ones have far too much hair," Alice says as she yanks out a whole clump and dumps it on the tea tray along with a bunch of dust.

"Do you realise you've got the handle of the Vax resting in the dog's water bowl?" Louise enquires mildly. This earns her such a filthy look from Alice that she actually recoils.

"Oh, look, I'm sorry," says Alice. "You must be Louise; nice to meet you properly at last. No, I wasn't annoyed with you, just with the God of Clean."

Even Araminta is baffled at this.

"Oh, it's from a short play I wrote when I was with Haringey Street Theatre in the early '70s. It was a polemic against the way advertising preyed on our fear of dirt in any shape or form. 'I am the God of Clean! I'm pristine, bright and pure…'"

Louise catches my eye, but I give her a stern look.

"Yes, the hygiene mania was even worse in those days," continues Alice.

"Remember 'Persil Washes Whiter'? You probably don't. A drawing of a dingy, ashamed looking kid next to a beaming, spotless one? And they had all those catch-phrases: 'the Understains' I remember was one of them. Oh yes, and 'Flocculent Filth'."

"So, what was Street Theatre like?" asks Louise.

"Oh, highly political! Left-wing, obviously—we were so dedicated that I remember once it was pouring with rain, and we still just went on performing, to literally no one."

She hauls the Vax upright, and as if to illustrate her story, the handle immediately gushes water all over the engine bit.

"That's not good," observes Araminta. "You could start a fire now if you turn that on."

Alice dabs it with a kitchen roll then gives up. "Look, I'll just bung it by the radiator; it'll be fine. Now, welcome, you two. Take a pew. Tea, coffee? Have a crumpet!"

I see, so not even beans on toast.

I'll make the ensuing conversation as if it was a play; it's just a lot easier.

ALICE: Now, I've asked you two here because I need your help. I've explained it all to Araminta; she's in the picture.

ARAMINTA: Basically, Alice hasn't had a single booking for her Airbnb since that woman Linda left that awful review. She basically couldn't stand the train noises—

ALICE: She said the toaster was filthy! My brand-new toaster! I could weep!

ME: Yes, I heard her say, "It's just not up to my standards!" I wasn't eavesdropping or anything...

ARAMINTA: Basically, she was livid because she'd pre-booked three whole stays all at once before she even got here, and Alice was only able to refund her half the money, cos once the calendar's blocked out, it's gone, and no one else can book it.

ALICE: (almost wailing) She said it smelled of damp! And the bread and milk were past their sell-by date! All absolute lies!

LOUISE: Yes, but don't you have any come-back?

ALICE: I could have written a review of her, but I thought *no, I wouldn't sink to her level.*

LOUISE: Big mistake.

ARAMINTA: And then, because she runs an Airbnb herself and knows all the tricks, she submitted her review just five minutes before the fourteen-day response window elapsed! So, there it stays, unchallenged.

ALICE: In all its glory.

ME: And you haven't had a single booking since?

ALICE: No, it's just dried up.

LOUISE: So, what's her Airbnb like? Just gonna have a look. Linda—Linda, what?

ALICE: Gledhill.

LOUISE: Wow, it's one of those. Looks brand new. Look at the main pic, very tasteful.

ME: Very John Lewis, isn't it, right down to the framed picture in the hallway of four feathers in a row—G-O-O-O-R-GEOUS!

LOUISE: OK, the reviews. "Linda is a really wonderful hostess; nothing was too much trouble." Hold on. "She made sure that my son had his favourite jam for breakfast."

ME: Ugh, she sounds almost saintly.

ARAMINTA: So, you two, as to why we invited you down—

ALICE: This is a council of war.

LOUISE: I suppose you've tried asking Airbnb to remove the said review?

ALICE: Oh, yes. I'm convinced it's just a series of robots one connects with, randomly choosing a few templates. It's all, "Thank you for reaching out to us!"

ME: But no joy?

ALICE: If you can believe it, they suggested I should thank the reviewer for their feedback, empathise with them and assure them that the issues will be improved.

This apparently has the power to 'disable the review' more effectively than 'further negativity'. Then they ended: 'And if you need further assistance, we will always be one step behind you'.

LOUISE: Creepy!

ME: Anyway, what's your plan? How do we fit in?

ALICE: (clears her throat nervously) Well, OK. I want you to go down there, to her perfect Airbnb, and sabotage it!

LOUISE: Sabotage it?

ALICE: I'd pay you!

ME: How much?

ALICE: I was thinking £100, not including the train fare to Hythe and the cost of the Airbnb.

LOUISE: We'll do it!

ME: Whoa, whoa, hold your horses – I'll do it, but only on the condition that my dogs are allowed to use your garden—like, once a day?

ALICE: That's three times the amount of poo—who's going to clear it up?

ME: Your cleaning lady?

ALICE: I haven't got a cleaning lady. You may be getting confused with Susie, my dog walker; she sometimes walks Deidre if my back's playing up.

ME: Oh yes, I've seen her in the street trying to control Deidre on the lead when she's rabid to get to the Common. Couldn't she do it?

Susie with Deidre the Dalmatian

ALICE: Certainly not! That's not in her remit. Except on the Common, obviously.

LOUISE: You need to have a word with yourself, Carla.

ME: It's just that I've seen the size of Deidre's poos; it's not a very enticing prospect.

ALICE: Haven't you heard of the latest method? It's called 'Stick and Flick'. No more messing around with poo bags; you just get a handy stick and launch it into the bushes! It's fun; you can imagine you're playing shove ha'penny on a cruise liner!

ME: Well, if it's so much fun, I wouldn't want to deprive you, Alice!

LOUISE: Oh, come on, Carla. Yes, she'll do it, Alice.

ME: OK, we'll take it in turns, then. You're Mondays; I'm Tuesdays, and so on. Is that OK? High five! And obviously, you'll have to look after my two when we're off doing your secret service job.

ALICE: Agreed.

It got even weirder after that. When we'd finally sorted out a date for this expedition, Alice then came up with the *coup de grace*, a small sealed bag of mouse droppings! I didn't like to ask where she got them from, but it was obvious what she wanted us to do with them. Sprinkle a few and then kick up an unholy fuss. Saint Linda well and truly screwed.

LOUISE: Where did you get hold of these droppings, Alice?

ALICE: Well, it wasn't easy, I've got ultrasonic anti-rodent bleepers in all the electrical sockets, so I just unplugged them all. Yes, I was even prepared to do that.

No Airbnb guests to worry about, of course.

LOUISE: Eww, that's gross! Couldn't you have just got some little—seeds? Like linseeds? They look just the same.

ME: Course not! Linda could just take them to be analysed or something.

ALICE: Exactly, Carla.

LOUISE: But then how did you get rid of the mice afterwards? (Vegan outrage about to explode any minute)

ALICE: Oh, they're actually very sweet. They were mainly in my food cupboard, gnawing little holes in the flour and sugar packets, so I just carefully cornered them, got them in a bucket and took them down to the Common, together with a little picnic I'd prepared to tide them over.

I honestly can't tell whether she's taking the piss or not. I think not. But anyway, I just never, never thought I'd ever agree to be part of something like this. I'm dreading it but also kind of looking forward to it, in equal measure. I suppose I get to see a nicer bit of the South coast than Margate—the only place I've been before—and maybe have a walk by the sea if there's time in between all the nefarious goings-on.

Alice

This scheme we've come up with – it's really not like me at all, to be all out for revenge.

But it's not just that Linda has removed a third of my income in a stroke; it's that I feel less of a person. I would feel hugely brought down if I just let this go, let her walk all over me. When I think about the two hours of cleaning I put in before her arrival, checking all the cereals, tea bags, coffee bags, fruit, fresh flowers—I put my heart and soul into it, I really did, well, like I always do—sincerely wanting to provide a nice experience for the guest, and taking pride in it. And then when someone tramples all over it, you feel like such a fool.

Chapter Nine

Carla

We've been summoned by Alice to finalise details for our trip. It's a dreary winter afternoon, and she does tea and crumpets for us again. Inevitably she embarks on another trip down memory lane, about the time she spent on the Kent coast about sixty years ago. It's kind of fascinating, in a gruesome way.

"Oh, I went to quite a few of those seaside towns—had my first kiss at a party in Broadstairs by the beach—I hated it! Horrible feeling, someone's tongue, wriggling around in your mouth, I still don't like it!"

The look on Louise's face is priceless.

"Do you know, Araminta and I were students in Canterbury at exactly the same time – I was at the art school, and she was teacher training. And we both did holiday jobs waitressing at Butlins in Margate in the summer of 1961, but we never met! Never knew each other. Well, that Butlins Dining Room was like an aircraft hangar."

"Did you enjoy the waitressing?" I ask.

"Parts of it! But you wouldn't believe how squalid the whole thing was. We had so many campers to serve, and the turnaround was so quick that you saw girls spitting on the plates to clean them, and you could score a line through the thick grime on the plastic tablecloths. The customers didn't seem to mind at all; they were being jollied along through the meal by the Redcoats, who kept yelling 'Hi de Hi!' and the whole room shouted back 'Ho de Ho!'"

Louise says, "Wow, I think I've seen a documentary of that time in black and white; they had a Knobbly Knees Competition by the pool. And a Miss Butlins Bathing Beauty prize—gross!"

"That's right. It seems so weird that I was actually there because, of course, my memories aren't in black and white at all. I remember the kitchen was boiling hot and full of fat men leaning against the wall with their flies open, lazily scratching their bollocks. No, these were the harmless ones! They were the ten percent on day release from local mental hospitals. It was the other ones you had to watch out for who refused to fill your plates unless they got a kiss. And all the food, including scrambled egg, was dolloped on to the plates by hand to save time. I remember there was a notice on the wall headed 'Breakfast Either/Or', then underneath, 'Two Tablespoons Cornflakes OR Three Prunes'."

"How much did you get paid for that job?" asks Louise.

"Three pounds a week!" (We can't help gasping.) "You had to make up the rest in tips. That's why the 'Kiss me or else!' blackmail was so effective."

"Sounds like the Seventh Circle of Hell." I comment.

"Well, it was certainly an Inferno. It was a hot summer anyway—we were dripping with sweat, and we had to carry two metal racks, one in each hand, with six loaded china plates in each one, then use our shoulders to push open the heavy swing doors.

"The diners had to slide out the plates and pass them around while we stood there. I had a name badge saying 'June' as they didn't have any Alices. I can still hear those people screeching in my dreams: 'June! June! June!'"

Alice is enjoying herself.

"I drank some bleach as well. Nobody cared!"

"W-H-A-A-T?" we chorus.

"Yes, it was in Robinson's Barley Water bottle. I was doing an extra shift in one of the Butlins Pubs and got really thirsty, so I thought I'd pinch a drink while the supervisor was in the loo – thank goodness I diluted it!"

"What happened?"

"I just couldn't breathe—my throat swelled up. The supervisor just yawned and said, 'If you're not feeling well, go to the doctor'. I drank gallons of water and just about survived, but my throat was really painful for days."

"God, nowadays, you'd probably get thousands in compensation," murmurs Louise.

"Wow, things were just so different in your time." I add. "Cos I was talking to Richard, your builder, he took his family to Butlins last summer and said it was fantastic with loads of facilities. Not the Margate one; he said that one closed down."

"Well, that was all those years ago. Margate is probably quite different now—absolutely spick and span and conforming to EU regulations—well, I know we're out of it now, but it had its effect. And all the regeneration, the new Turner Gallery—it must be on the up!"

I'm going back to the 'play' format.

ME: Well, that's what you'd think, but I was down there last month for a gig, and it was even worse! The gig was great, in a really cute venue called the Tom Thumb Theatre, but then

I walked along the cliff road to this hotel I'd booked called Bay View, run by Egyptians—

LOUISE: You can't say that!

ME: Can't say what?

LOUISE: Egyptians! It's racist!

ME: Oh, all right (Never get into an argument with her.) It was run by a family from North Africa. A very smart reception area, where they took your payment on a card.

So, then I was given a key and told to go up three flights of narrow stairs and opened the door into a tiny room where the end of the bed was touching the basin, and you had to walk sideways to get between the bed and the chest of drawers. It was icy cold, being February, and then I noticed that a whole pane of glass was missing from the window, and the gap had been stuffed with rolled-up newspapers! It made the non-stop seagulls even louder. I tugged open one drawer and found it full of dirty breakfast plates with solidified egg and ketchup smears and cutlery to match. The worst thing was that the plug was stuck fast in the basin, so you couldn't use it at all.

ALICE: So, what on earth did you do?

ME: Well, there was a house phone, so I rang down and explained, and they sent the son of the family up. Now, this I wasn't expecting, he was absolutely gorgeous, he looked like a young Omar Sharif—

LOUISE: Racist!

ME: With long eyelashes. He seemed nice, too, eager to help. He rolled his sleeves up, but he couldn't shift the plug either, so he reached into the drawer and got one of the eggy forks to see if that would do any good. I was just watching him, the muscles in his arms and shoulders—

LOUISE: Bet he wondered what he'd got himself into—being ogled by this middle-aged woman.

ME: Well, be that as it may, I ended up being upgraded to a huge double room.

ALICE: Really? What did you do to achieve that?

ME: I really wouldn't like to say. Let's just say a good time was had by all…

LOUISE: What, in the horrid room or the upgraded room?

ME: Right there in the horrid room, next to the greasy plates and forks.

(Alice seems to be looking at me with new respect.)

ALICE: And was the new room all right?

ME: The window panes were all intact, at least. The basin had no plug at all, but I could live with that. The bathroom, one flight down, was a nightmare. I noticed this odd pattern all over the bath and suddenly realised it was little curls of black pubic hair!

LOUISE: Racist!

ME: And there was only cold water. The loo didn't flush. And there was a hole in the window taped over with cardboard.

LOUISE: Well, at least you got a bedroom upgrade, I suppose.

ME: The next morning, I was really looking forward to breakfast, which was included. I had visions of a lovely hot plate of bacon, sausage, egg and mushrooms with hot coffee.

LOUISE: Uh-oh…

ME: Mm, yes, I had to go down to this freezing basement. There was absolutely nobody there; on a side table were a pile of white sliced bread, a plate of white peeled hardboiled eggs, a jar of instant coffee, a kettle and some powdered milk. And a dead spider.

ALICE: To look on the bright side, prisoners in Auschwitz would have killed for that!

Louise looks like she's debating whether to say 'Racist!' or not.

ME: Are you Jewish, Alice?

ALICE: No, not at all, but I always try to see the upside of everything. Count one's blessings, kind of thing.

ME: Oh, and then five minutes later, I got joined by a homeless man who'd been put in the hotel by the local council. So, I had someone to talk to, at least.

LOUISE: Did you bonk him too?

ME: Well, no. He was far from appetising.

ALICE: I think you'll find Hythe quite different. Anyway, back to the matter in hand—no second thoughts?

LOUISE: No way. Well, I think Carla's a bit conflicted – good job, she's got me to stiffen her sinews like Lady M in the Scottish play! But I've been wondering: why did you want me along on this, Alice? Was it because of the booking?

ALICE: Oh, I thought you realised. Yes, I asked you to book it because of your address—completely untraceable to my one!

ME: You see, that's the side of it I don't like—the whole thing seems really devious and dishonest.

ALICE: It has to be in order to work! You'd be surprised how much necessary subterfuge there is in all reaches of society.

LOUISE: Yeah! Totally agree! Politicians—big business—

ME: Yes, but not nurses…or firefighters…or the police, for that matter—

ALICE: Ha! You'd be surprised. Let me tell you: when Benjy was at the local primary school, Henry Claverley—

ME: Is this another of your anecdotes, Alice?

ALICE: Just a very short one. Just to illustrate my point. The playground was all very open in those days—about twenty-five years ago—not like now, it's Fort Knox. The kids were all milling about, and a car drew up by the gate and offered sweets and a lovely drive around to any takers—well, three or four kids didn't need asking twice and bundled in. Later in the day, there was going to be a talk given by the local police. So, everyone gathered in the hall, and the guest police officer, with a great flourish, singled out the kids who'd got in the car and heaped every kind of shame on their heads—turned out the whole thing had been a hoax by the Wandsworth Police! Give the children an object lesson they'd never forget!

LOUISE: Jesus fucking Christ! Pardon my French.

ME: Are you sure, Alice? I'm sure something like that would be in the public domain.

ALICE: You'd think so, wouldn't you, but I think that's part of the web of deceit, or perhaps just a papering-over-the-cracks decorum – those things tend to get covered up and forgotten. They just linger on in the memories of old crones like me – oh, and I expect Benjy and his contemporaries. Perhaps even they are beginning to think they imagined it.

LOUISE: It's a kind of Theatre in the Community!

ME: Well, at least that puts tomorrow's escapade in the shade a bit. Quite looking forward to it, in a way!

LOUISE: Hurrah!

Chapter Ten

Carla

"Don't do that!" Louise cries, kind of swatting at my hands. I could deck her; I really could. It's so humiliating! Plus, she's assuming an unwarranted level of familiarity with me. We're on the train down to Hythe, it's actually happening, and I'm so bored I'm picking away at the skin around my fingernails. Childhood habit. She's right, though; mangled fingers is not a good look.

She's been lost to her phone since we boarded at Waterloo, no doubt Facebooking her out-of-work actor friends. The train seems to stop at a station every ten minutes: Paddock Wood, Staplehurst, Headcorn, Pluckley—to think people actually live in these places! We should have gone from Kings Cross, it takes half an hour instead of an hour and a half, but it seems Alice's purse wouldn't stretch to that. Anyway, at least we don't have to change anywhere. I googled the station we have to alight at and found a trove of comedy gold: "Sandling Station Carpark is the top dogging hotspot of East Kent." This is followed by a hilarious chat-room peopled by actual Kentish doggers. "Are you sure it's there? I turned left at Newing Green as you said, but just ended up back on the motorway!"

That was last night; I'm not feeling so hilarious today. I've got the equivalent of pre-gig nerves about this, feeling more and more awful as we approach our destination. I totally wish I hadn't agreed to this—why did I? It's wrong, on any level, and I'm sure there's going to be some form of karmic retribution. It's as though the gods are looking down, weighing up all the good and evil in the world, like two giant sacks on each end of a seesaw. And our prank will be the one thing that unleashes the wrath of the gods on the whole entire world—plagues of locusts, frogs raining from a bruised and darkened sky...

"Feeling OK?" asks Louise. "You look a bit peaky—fancy one of Alice's Rescue Remedy pastilles?" (A last-minute good luck gift.)

"Just got a bad feeling about this."

"Mate! You were the one who said, 'Be more Countess Bathory!' Put your money where your mouth is! We're nearly there, anyway."

Oh god, here we are at Sandling; it certainly doesn't look like a den of iniquity. It's the picture of a country station from the 1930s, completely unspoilt, with lovely trees, little daffodils, and absolutely no one around. The taxi we ordered, however, is bang on time. "88, North Down, please!" Louise clutches my arm, her face one huge grin of excitement. "Bring it on!" She turns to me. "Got the you-know-what?"

I nod.

Alice

I can't help feeling a bit apprehensive about this, now that they've set off. I suddenly realised that today's date 3-02-2020, when added up, is figure nine.

As in the Nine of Spades! Terribly unlucky. That song from the popular version of Carmen, Carmen Jones, (my favourite) keeps running through my head:

'Da nine!
Da here's—de old boy
Plain as can be
Death got his hand – on ME.'

Oh well.

Carla

"Now what?" We're both sitting in our first-floor room in Linda's Airbnb, yes, room rather than rooms, #skinflintAlice, and the rain is lashing at the window. I can see that normally you'd get a bit of a sea view in between the chimney tops, but it's all misted over.

"Well, I don't really fancy a walk along the prom. I should think you'd get blown over," I observe.

"I have to say, I think Linda's got a nerve complaining about trains when we've had seagulls screeching ever since we got here," adds Louise.

Thank God we don't have to share that hard-looking double bed. We'll be out of here by then, having done the dirty deed and heading off to a cheap hotel that Alice forked out for. (That could be even worse.) Is she gay? Linda, I mean—

I got the impression she had us down for a couple of lesbians and was almost too friendly; showed us an extremely compact breakfast area in a small kitchen next to a teeny backyard. She offered us 'the full English' for tomorrow's breakfast, or "'Continental'—by the way, on a good day, you can see France out of your window upstairs! Oh yes, of course, we've got Wi-Fi—don't worry if you can't get a signal, you can usually get one by the window in the bathroom."

The bathroom's got a massive bath and a rather plasticky-looking freestanding shower, nothing to write home about. Framed watercolours of boats, and little painted wooden lighthouses, a plethora of seaside kitsch. 'Sparkling clean', as per Airbnb's sacred mantra. I'm taking plenty of photos to satisfy Alice's insatiable curiosity.

"This is going to be a problem with the mouse droppings; they'll probably fall down between the wooden floorboards." I remark.

"Hold on a sec," hisses Louise, jumping up from the bed to look out the window. I rush over, and we see Linda exiting the property with a man! They have an animated conversation—the guy (a real bruiser) has a booming laugh.

When suddenly—for some reason—the guy looks up and clocks us both, staring at him! It's a horrible moment because his laugh cuts off, and his eyes seem to bore into us for a second. I instantly pretend to be looking out to sea while Louise ducks down, which I feel is a mistake. Oh crikey.

We hear Linda coming back in. We decide to have a coffee, which has a bit of a catering coffee taste and watch EastEnders for a bit on the wall-mounted TV. This is rather too big for the room, so everything seems a touch blurry, or is it just my nerves?

Half an hour later, we both seem to agree that we've been there long enough.

We can hear her clattering about in the kitchen, so it's now or never. I unpack the plastic bag of mouse droppings—the only thing that does get unpacked—and carefully scatter it slightly behind the bed and trying to get a little bit on the rug.

However, Louise is lifting up the edge of the rug as if trying to decide whether it's genuine Turkish or just from Argos; "Hang on!" She yelps. "There's a whacking great hole under here! She can probably hear what we're saying; keep your voice down!"

"Take a pic of that hole straight away, Louise! Cos, don't you see, of course there'd be mice, that's where they come up!"

"Their means of ingress is how we shall word it, Carla."

She drops the rug corner, and I do some further judicious sprinkling.

"Does that look natural?"

"How the fuck would I know? Now quick, let's both get some photos. Put the bedside light on."

To be honest, I'm feeling terrible when I'm doing all this—I have to keep reminding myself what a vicious bitch Linda was to Alice.

"Right, let's go! This shouldn't be too hard; I'm an actress, and you're supposed to be a comedian. We're both genuinely shocked—somewhat sad and regretful, but struggling to control our deep, visceral revulsion—"

"Yes, yes, I get it! You'd better do the talking then as you're the listed guest."

We head off down the polished wooden stairs—actually not a bad feature—with our coats and backpacks on and meet

Linda coming out of the kitchen with an enquiring look on her face.

"Off out? Is everything all right?"

"Well, no, not, as it happens Linda, I'm really sorry, I don't know how to tell you this, but we can't stay! We're going to have to leave! The thing is, I'm really sorry, Linda, but there are some rat faeces behind the bed."

"Rat faeces?" Linda's face has gone ashen; she appears to have aged ten years in a second."

Linda Undone

"Well, more like mouse droppings, I'd say." I suggest.

"No—no—that's simply not possible—let me just—" Linda cries.

"We're just going to have to leave, I'm afraid," states Louise firmly. "You've been very welcoming, but you see, I've got an allergy to rodents anyway; we don't seem to get rats or mice in Streatham, thankfully. OK, we'll be off then. I've taken photos of the droppings if you want to see them?"

She fishes out her camera and holds it out to Linda, but Linda has sort of collapsed on to a sofa, and I start pushing Louise out the door, dropping the key on to a table—and we're out into the cold, drizzly, blowy little road and heading down a very steep incline to our hotel in the High Street. My heart's going nineteen to the dozen; Louise is giggling hysterically.

Most of the way down is alongside a vast, grassy graveyard with a massive church looming up in the middle of it. You literally have to hold on to the handrail; it's that steep and slippery with the rain actually cascading down the slope.

It's a relief to get to the High Street, although when we get to the Swan and Cygnet, we have to stand at the bar for ages before anyone notices us: it's packed with bucolic men bawling their heads off. Then when we finally get the key to our room, 'Romney Marsh.'

No one bothers to show us up. We have to exit into the rain again to a dismal back yard where cigarette butts are bobbing around in a puddle, then re-enter and go up some poky stairs to a freezing room containing two narrow beds, a table, a chair and a TV.

"Christ, no one's been in here for a decade," mutters Louise.

"Put the telly on; it might give off some heat," I suggest.

"Telly's buggered too!" Hectic fuzzy zigzags and unbearable noise. "You'll have to go and get someone," she says.

"No way! Not going outside again. Look, there's a massive bath here, let's try the water—cold of course—oh, hold on, no, it's OK, it's getting hot. We could warm up in the bath and then just go to bed. You go first if you like; I'll try and make a cup of tea with that kettle."

So that's what we agree to do. I'm feeling very, very strange, partly because of the night's events but also because the floor in here actually slopes: walking to the bathroom, you have a weird sensation of walking uphill, and it's not like I've got any energy left!

After our baths, we dine on some left-over vegan sandwiches Louise got at Waterloo and then climb into bed wondering if we'll ever fall asleep, what with the damp sheets and the howling draught through the window.

"Well, this is fun!" I groan. "Right now, all I can see is a massive beefburger, dripping with meat juices and onions—not a hippy-drippy pussy liberal loser burger that tastes of being 'woke!'"

All I get in return is a loud snore. No, she's actually gone to sleep.

I should think this is probably the worst night of my life.

I've actually managed to fall asleep in spite of everything. I dream I'm in my mother's kitchen, which has a vast, sloping cobbled floor. I open the fridge door hungrily, and several things fall straight out.

"Yes, I need to get that fridge seen to," says my mum.

"No! It's the sloping floor!" I cry, having a light bulb moment. "Cos it's the same with the cooker—unless you shut the door really quickly. Straightening up this floor could be a good use of your money!"

She giggles. "I can think of more entertaining ways of using my money!"

"But every time you open the fridge, the fucking contents go all over the floor!"

My dad frowns. He doesn't like swearing, and besides, there's a troop of black Christians filing into the room, which is now a Pentecostal Church. He opens his mouth, and a sound like the knell of doom blares out.

I explode awake. It's a fire alarm, so loud it almost blots out the universe.

"Oh, Jesus fucking Christ," moans Louise. "Are you shitting fucking serious?"

We're scrambling to put our coats and shoes on.

"I'm taking the duvet down as well!" Louise says, grabbing them both and giving me one as we stumble out the door to see other people emerging from rooms in various stages of undress. In the grimy backyard, a hotel guy is waving us back through the pub and out into the street. At least it's stopped raining. There's quite a crowd, some bleary, others looking quite excited, and most having copied our idea of clutching duvets, or in some cases, towels, around themselves. There's a buzz of conversation, which almost seems to turn into a bit of a party atmosphere.

"Where's the fire, then? False alarm, is it?"

"Can I get back to my forty winks, officer?" This to a couple of policemen who've now arrived on the scene.

"At the end of the day, sir, we can't let you back in till the building's been fully evacuated, now can we, sir?"

Denis 'Boy' Boynton

At this, the most extraordinary bunch of people spew out of the hotel's main entrance.

"Bloody hell, won't you take a look at that," murmurs Louise, nudging my arm.

It's two burly tattooed men wearing nothing but silky shorts and bright red boxers' robes, complete with boxing gloves with which they are jovially sparring the air and each other. Alongside the pair is a phalanx of gorgeous, skimpily-dressed women – my first thought is *gangsters' molls!*

I hear a woman next to me, telling her husband: "Oh yes, they always have these fights here, all through February— they start at midnight and carry on till dawn. It's down in the basement, so it doesn't worry anyone."

One of the floozies asks Louise for a light. They start chatting and smoking together, so I join in—better than just standing here bored to death. Turns out this girl, who's really friendly and called Shazza, has a gig serving drinks and stuff to the fight punters. She got the job online, I imagine because she looks the part, but she's an actress like Louise and also from Streatham, like Louise! I'm telling her I live in Balham and all about my stand up, and she says she's thinking of giving it a go. "You and the rest of the world..." I feel like saying but manage not to. Then, as Louise is telling her about an Ionesco play she was in at the Marlowe, Canterbury, I suddenly get a horrible feeling that I'm being watched. I look up and see a pair of eyes drilling into me – it's one of the boxers, but it's also the same guy who was outside Linda's Airbnb in North Down!

Just a weird coincidence, I suppose, but I put my hood up and pretend to be engrossed in a shop called Church Mouse with lots of watercolours of boats and miniature lighthouses, tiny seagulls suspended above on wires. Déjà vu, or what.

Shazza

Alice

I couldn't get to sleep last night: I was certain the girls would be ringing or texting me with "Mission accomplished" or something; it really was intensely frustrating. Still, when they arrived back here around midday, looking somewhat dishevelled and exhausted, I could understand the reason for no message. They'd slept the entire way back on the train, and they seemed to be hinting that £50 each wasn't quite enough for all they'd been through, so I threw in a couple of almost full bottles of wine and a box of Thornton's left over from Christmas. Araminta had hurried over too, so I heated up some soup, and we sorted out the wording for our message to Airbnb on the app, complete with incriminating photographs. I can't help congratulating myself on the mouse droppings idea because I'd carefully studied the rules and regs, and anything to do with bugs, infestations, or rodents is just a complete no-no; you can get all of your money back plus *carte blanche* to write a no-holds-barred review which really will cook Linda's goose if you don't mind a few mixed metaphors!

The girls seemed not too interested once they'd got their money, seemed to be itching to get away and 'crash', but I made sure that Louise, who I can't help feeling is slightly more clued up than our Carla, and whose name was on the booking, had sent off the message to Airbnb. A message as if written by a genuinely nice, well-meaning person who felt really, very sorry at having to cancel the stay, but really, one did have to maintain some standards in life and mice in the bedroom was just one step too far.

As I say, Linda's goose—well and truly cooked. It has a nice ring to it.

Chapter Eleven

Carla

A week's gone by since Airbnb gate. I haven't seen much of Alice, but when I do, she's like the cat that got the cream. She keeps asking me to check Linda's calendar for bookings (she couldn't do it herself without revealing her identity), and I'm able to report back. "It's like Old Mother Hubbard's cupboard!" or "It's like the Gobi Desert!" Alice's pestering is quite annoying—interrupting me when I'm trying to write my new set on dogging.

Louise has also kept her in the loop about the torrent of messages she's had from Linda, alternating from pleading to threatening on a daily basis, but as per instructions, she's replied to them all with sweetly sad variations of "I'm afraid it was what it was, Linda!"

Now Louise just wants it to stop and regrets ever getting involved. So, to cheer her up, I've asked her to be my plus one tonight at the Stockwell Arms, though, of course, it's actually her doing me a favour, and several drinks will have to be coming her way.

I'm desperate to try out my new 'dogging' material, inspired by Sandling Station—at least I got something out of that expedition!

This is a notorious night which has been going on for donkey's years with a beautiful room they call 'The Ballroom', always with a cracking audience, down to the 'plus one' rule, which means the gig is called 'a bringer'. A bringer gig is absolute anathema to a lot of comedians, and the various online comedy forums have at least one thread a day of comics trying to outdo each other in their mockery and condemnation of the practice. However, only too often the alternative (at least at an open-mic level) seems to be to perform just to the other comedians on the line-up and perhaps two 'real audience' who've wandered in off the street.

The promoter MC of this night, Rory Rossiter, is well-known for being 'woke;' he has an 'Ethos' for the night, which consists of a long list of rules: you can't 'punch down', be any sort of 'ist' except feminist, or leave before the night's over. Unusually for comedians, he's an Oxford graduate, coruscatingly bright and well-informed: the thought of him makes me even more nervous on top of my usual pre-gig nerves, so on arrival, I head straight for the toilet. It's a unisex loo—part of the egalitarian vibe—with a urinal next to the hand-washing basin and two cubicles.

From one of the cubicles, which is closed, issue forth loud baritone tuning-up exercises. I suspect it's Rory. On the inside of my cubicle is a notice: "Please urinate only in this toilet." The singing stops. There's a deathly silence, and I immediately get total bladder paralysis: conscious that there's someone a foot away from me, listening.

With every fibre of my being, I eventually force out a ridiculous-sounding trickle, and then Rory's voice booms out: "I don't know what you're planning to do in there, but that toilet is only for peeing."

"Yes, thanks, I saw the notice," I reply meekly—possibly the most embarrassing start to a gig ever.

Here at the Stockwell Arms, it used to be that Rory would pick a numbered comedian at random from his clipboard, so every single time, it could be you next, leading to surging adrenalin over and over again—horrible it was. But this time, it's far more humane, and I'm third in the running order; fantastic, that's always my lucky sweet spot.

Rory Rossiter

Rory kicks the night off on good form – he's a one-off, nerdy and a little mad. It's really hard to listen to the first two acts, as the words of my new set are running obsessively through my head—but at last, it's me. I'm in character as a timid housewife who gets led astray.

"Hell-o-o-o-o! Let's get one thing out the way, right? I'm Carla Capstick, and I'm up for grabs! No, not like that, just as in—anything I can do to help: charity fund-raising, cupcakes, traybakes…the other day, I was just staring into the goblet of my Magimix—it was a positive blizzard of buttercream—and my friend Louise came in. She was just watching me—watching the blizzard of buttercream—and she said, 'You look like a fucking retard – when was the last time you had a life?' (Got a laugh.)

"'I've decided! We're both going to go on the razz!'

"(Doubtfully). 'The razz?'

"'Yes, the razz! You know, the razzle! Predatory elderly women, on the prowl, for fresh meat—down Balham High Road!'

"'Oh no, I couldn't do that! I'm on the Parish Council!' (Big laugh.)

"'Oh well, in that case, I've got a much better idea: we're going to go dogging. In your old Morris Minor!'

"'What's that?'

"'Dogging? It's Britain's top leisure-time activity—after badger-baiting and tax evasion—we'll be bang on trend! And, plus, it's a hundred percent respectable—it's an ancient, noble British tradition dating all the way back to Chaucer'.

"'Oh well, if you put it like that, it's almost unpatriotic not to join in'." (Laugh.)

Yes, looked at one way, stand up is one big ego-trip, but if it gives you a buzz to get laughs and people coming up to you saying nice things, that's understandable, isn't it? One thing I've sometimes got praise for is seeming to include the whole audience by roaming my eyes around and not just staring straight ahead.

Except for this time, I get a horrible shock because there, suddenly, staring fixedly at me, I see, sitting together, Linda and the boxer guy from the Swan and Cygnet, the one who gave me the evils. I nearly drop the mic; it's so spooky and so unexpected.

My mouth's instantly gone as dry as a bone, but somehow, I struggle on to the end and even get some laughs. Definitely not going to win the Stockwell Cup in the clap-off tonight, but I think I may have bigger problems.

At the break, when everyone repairs to the bar, Louise and I decide to make a break for it, although it's strictly against the house rules not to stay to the end, and it may end up with me being blacklisted here.

"How could they have found us?" Louise whines as we scurry to get into the Morris.

"Well, I've worked it out! You only went and told the waitress girl your name! And she knows the boxer guy— Linda's pal! He looks as mean as fuck too!"

"Hold on! You told her you were from Balham and your name! They've only got to Facebook you, there you are, they know what you look like, and there are all your gigs listed!"

"Oh fuck, they must be putting two and two together, maybe, that Alice is behind our scam!"

"Yes, well, look, there's a car right behind us, that grey one—I think it's them!" Louise squeaks. "Can't you go any faster?" We're going at quite a lick down Bolingbroke Road by this time.

"Don't be ridiculous, this is a Morris Minor, and that looks like a Ford Fiesta. Anyway, this is a 20-mph zone, and I got a hefty fine for doing 30 down here once before—"

"Well, what are we going to do? You can't just go home; seems like they're pretty determined to stick to us like glue. And let's face it, it's not really our problem, is it? We fulfilled our side of the bargain; let's just go to yours as planned." Oh lord...

Alice

Gosh—feeling a little flat now—yes, it was a victory but, somehow, less satisfying than I'd imagined. Life's subsided to the point of being quite humdrum – what's it all about? Somehow, I thought that getting my own back on Linda would herald a bright new dawn, be a bit of a turning point. It reminds me of a woman called Beryl, who was on my postgraduate Art Teacher Training Course. Although she was a mature student—well, possibly in her fifties—she tried to fit in with the rest of the students and worked much harder than most of us. One day we'd been told to take prints and impressions from our urban environment, and she came across a beautiful rainbow in a slick of motor oil. I remember how delighted she was as she rushed to lay a piece of paper over it and how disappointed with the dirty smear it yielded.

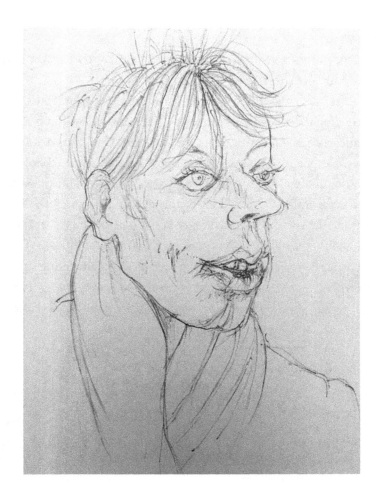

Benjy

Twenty years later, Benjy, as a baby, reached out to touch a ray of sunlight and then licked his hand eagerly. No buttery taste, then! I really felt for him.

The worst of it is, Benjy and Liliana are now talking about relocating to LA! What?

No! and if they do, they'll be gone even before Mother's Day!

Araminta's currently washing her hair in my shower as her boiler's broken down.

I'm just sitting here. I'm watching a tiny bug navigate the vast expanse of the wooden floor. I can't even make out if it's a microscopic spider or an ant. But the one thing that always mystifies me is, what on earth is it doing? Does anyone know? It's chugging along with such a sense of purpose, almost as if it's got a train to catch, then it does a 360 and energetically retraces its route before suddenly veering off to the right. Is it lost? What's going on? Is it foraging for a family? Is it a teenager leaving home with its first taste of adventure and freedom? Either way, the idea of a careless stomping boot or a tsunami wave (if it's in the shower) takes on tragic proportions in my mind. Am I going mad?

And the inescapable thought—*does my life really have any more meaning than this ant scenario*? And an even more lowering realisation that my reflections are entirely unoriginal; Shakespeare's been there first:

> 'And the poor beetle that we tread upon
> In corporal sufferance finds a pang as great
> As when a giant dies.'
> (Measure for Measure). Also:

> 'As flies to wanton boys are we to the gods,
> They kill us for their sport.'
> (King Lear.)

I think I need a drink.

Chapter Twelve

Carla

I don't think I've ever been 'tailed' before. There's a first time for everything!

It's impossible to stay calm: I blurt: "You do realise we could be leading a murderer directly to Alice? They'd probably polish off Araminta as well; she's usually there on a Tuesday night."

I'm pretending that I'm reviewing the options, but really, I'm in panicked auto-pilot mode and have actually arrived in my road, complete with grey Fiesta still on our heels.

I park but not directly outside the house. It suddenly occurs to me that I needn't have bothered; they've got all the information they need. They get out of their car in double-quick time and head for the house.

"Oh, god! Quick! What do we do? Louise? Shall we run away or go to yours? No, we can't! Besides, my dogs are in there!"

"Well, I'm not missing this for anything! Come on!" She jumps out and starts sprinting for the house, with me stumbling after her.

We can hear Alice's annoying doorbell repeatedly chiming in the night air. As I go through the gate, the front door suddenly yawns open, and Alice is on the doorstep slightly breathless, all three dogs milling around her legs and barking. "All right! All right! Where's the fire? What on earth? Linda? What? Why are you here? And who's your friend? Is this anything to do with you, Carla?"

The burly pugilist speaks up for the first time, squaring up to Alice: "I'll be asking the questions tonight, Madam, if you don't mind!"

He has quite a squeaky voice. His sheer bulk is intimidating, though, and he seems to have muscled his way into the hall. The dogs give him an enthusiastic welcome.

"Wait a minute, you, what do you think you're doing?" Alice cries indignantly.

"Through here, is it? Come on, Linda!" They push their way into Alice's kitchen, and it's all starting to feel a bit scary. Alice lurches after them, and we take up the rear. The kitchen is empty: Araminta must be late.

Alice grabs up her phone. "I'm ringing the police; you can't just—" Burly Man dashes it to the floor. All the dogs start barking like crazy, and he has to shout above the din.

"Oh no, you don't! I think you'll find you owe us an explanation, and we're not leaving till we get it! And don't you try anything either, you girls, I'm watching you! Horrible little trouble-makers the lot of you. But you'll pay for what you've done. Oh, yes."

Linda stands there looking smug and triumphant.

"I don't think we've been introduced," says Alice to the boxer.

"Ha! Well, that's neither here nor there, but I'm known as Denis 'Boy' Boynton, winner of this year's East Kent

96

Heavyweight title. Also known informally as Denny Damage."

"He inflicts damage." Linda pipes up.

"But only when it's deserved," adds Denis. "You can all sit down now!" We do.

At this point, the toilet door bursts open—it's Araminta, with crazy Medusa hair! Denis wheels around in surprise. Araminta must have been listening through the door because she's armed herself with a sink plunger and is halfway through a lunge at Denis when someone presses the 'Freeze' button—she freezes. "Denise?" she says. What. The. Actual. Fuck.

"Mrs Barnwell!" Denis cries. They rush up to each other and shake hands warmly; they're close to hugging. "I'm not Denise anymore; it didn't take. I'm back to being Denis," he tells her.

"Mrs Barnwell was my careers adviser at Brockshill Academy in Hythe," he tells us. He seems to have abandoned his threatening persona altogether. "She was my favourite teacher and helped me through a really hard time. Gender issues…she even introduced me to the Women's Boxing League."

"So, Denis, I'm sorry it didn't work out for you, I really am," says Araminta.

"Yes, well, long story short, it was never going to work. I was fed up with all the sniggers, they're not very 'woke' in Hythe, and I am six foot tall and big built. They didn't like it when I kept winning the women's trophies. Then my wife Dianne kicked me out because she couldn't bear the pitying looks she got. She made it super-hard for me to see the kids as well. I ended up on the streets—homeless."

"Surely that's not allowed in Hythe, though, is it?" asks Araminta. "Not even on the beach, I hear…"

Denis on the Circle Line

"You're right. I had to come up to London. Spent most of the time kipping on the Circle Line. You could do that then— don't know about now. But then I met this wonderful person Linda—"

"Where did you meet? On the Circle Line?" enquires Louise.

"Oh, no! At Hythe Spiritualist Temple, when I was down trying to visit my kids – Linda's a healer!"

"A healer?" says Louise.

"Yes, Louise," says Linda. "People do say I seem to have the touch, harnessing the power of music, as well."

"She was there to teach us some amazing chants; it was so empowering," muses Denis.

"Could we hear one?" Louise asks Linda, catching my eye.

"Oh no, not now. Well, if Denis joins in."

The rhythm of it sounds like a tribe of Apache Indians dancing with drums around a campfire.

> "I am a strong woman
> I am a holy woman
> I am a hea-ea-ler—
> My soul will never die-ie!"

"How does that go again?" I enquire. Louise and I are both trying to keep a straight face and also to memorise the chant for future use. "Have you got a pen, Alice?"

So, they do it again with even more fervour and with us two joining in. We all clap at the end.

"Well, you did ask!" says Denis, a little flushed with embarrassment but mainly pleased. "Just so you know…" He continues a little forlornly. "I may go on life's journey as Denis, but I'll always be a woman inside. And Linda helps me; she understands."

We absorb this in sympathetic silence.

"Look, before you continue, how about we crack open a bottle of wine?" asks Alice. What's come over her? She gets to her feet, but in the end, it's me and Louise, who do the pouring and handing around.

"Cheers! Now, where was I? Telling you my life story, aren't I? So dear Linda offered to let me sleep in her shed." He intercepts a look between Louise and me.

"It's not how it sounds: it's fully kitted out with light, heat and water. But anyway, Mrs Barnwell—"

"Please call me Araminta now!"

"Araminta then—and Alice, is it? Look, I'm sorry for the strong-arm tactics, Alice; how's your phone?"

"It's fine, as a matter of fact. Look, I keep it in this protective rubber casing!"

Yes, she does. It looks like a slab of gristle.

"That's a relief. I don't want to be seen as some sort of thug. Let's just put our cards on the table, all of us. Linda told me what happened, the scam with the mouse-droppings, and she was so devastated. Then later, the penny dropped that I'd seen these two young ladies twice, once at Linda's, spying on me from the window, and then again at that fire drill. I remembered that Shazza'd been chatting to them, and I pieced it together when she said one of them was from Balham. And because I owe Linda big-time, we did a bit more detective work, and now here we are!"

"I see," says Araminta uncertainly.

Denis turns to Alice. "If you'll forgive me for saying so, it would have been so much better if you'd just bitten the bullet and let Linda off all the money."

"Yes, like that was ever going to happen." I observe.

"What do you mean, Carla?" asks Alice.

"Well, you are quite careful with money—"

"What do you mean? I have to be!"

"No, I mean, well, now that everyone's baring their souls and everything—you do sort of take it to the next level—"

"Go on," says Alice in a sort of gritted teeth way.

"Yes, entertain us!" Louise interjects. "You can imagine it's a comedy night; I mean, there are almost enough of us to be the typical audience..."

"Well, say there was a lock-down and a food shortage like in China with that virus, you'd be the first one to be squeezing out old teabags to re-use them!" (She probably does already.)

"Entirely based on supposition!" Louise cries. "We'll never know the answer to that one unless Alice relocates to Wuhan Province!"

"I hate to say this," says Denis, "but a Facebook friend of mine, he's a boxer called Li Xhing Pi, says that that virus is going to spread worldwide. Probably."

"Oh, just when we were starting to enjoy ourselves," says Araminta.

"Yeah, give it a rest, Denis," adds Louise somewhat rudely.

"Whilst I admit to the improbability of a global pandemic." I resume, ignoring Louise's "Give it a rest, Carla!"

"I have, as a matter of fact, got visual proof of Alice's parsimony closer to home."

"Someone's swallowed a dictionary!" Linda chirps.

"Do you want to hear this or not? I'll take your silence to mean yes."

"Well…" I begin. "Last summer, I saw you several times on the Common when we both happened to be walking our dogs, and you were bending down every so often and digging up clumps of the park grass. You even had a trowel and a carrier bag, so it was obviously something you'd planned."

Linda's mouth is hanging open at this point.

"Then, later on, I could see you out of my upstairs window carefully transplanting the lumps of grass on to bare patches on your, well, um 'lawn'. That's not unusual behaviour at all, is it?"

Linda's face is now turning more into an expression of pity. Whereas, Alice is starting to giggle.

"I had to admire your perseverance." I conclude. "You seemed to be at it nearly every day, but the 'lawn' never looked any less patchy and bare, plus it was all different lengths!"

It must be my comic delivery, aided by Alice's infectious giggle because now everyone is laughing.

"Oh my!" Alice gasps. "You're so right about me scrimping and saving and cutting corners; I just can't help it. It was the way I was brought up; I suppose. I mean, for example, in a TV drama, you see a young lady, or young wife, cook a delicious dinner for her lover or husband, but he never comes! The hours' drag on agonisingly—he never shows up! And it always, always ends with the delicious dinner being shovelled into a pedal-bin! What a waste!"

"Well, I think it's supposed to be a symbolic gesture, isn't it?" Louise suggests.

"No, but I mean, the dogs could have it! At the very least. Whenever I see that—and it happens a lot—"

"Yes. It's a trope or meme." Louise confirms, showing off her drama school training.

"I always think—spoilt bitch! In her spotless kitchen! I always want to reach into that pedal bin and retrieve the lovely poached salmon or whatever."

"Not a good idea," mutters Linda.

"And as for—" Alice is warming to her theme. "Flowers! Don't get me started on that! Some awful philanderer or suspected child murderer with a few quid to spare brings around or has delivered, in an effort to clear his name, a huge exquisite bouquet—scented stocks, creamy lilies—"

102

"Yes, yes, we get the picture." I sigh.

"In the bin! In the bin! All of them! Just squash them in, break all the stems!"

"There should really be a disclaimer, I suppose. 'No flowers were hurt in the making of this movie,'" says Louise, rolling her eyes.

"Yes! That's exactly how I feel. To be honest, though, I have to admit to a special obsession with grass: do you know, when I first moved in here, in 1986, the garden was even worse than it is now. So, whenever the other mums from my Natural Childbirth Trust Group came for tea, I'd mow the grass and then sprinkle all the cuttings on top of the bare patches. It looked almost convincing from a distance—but what would you have done, Linda?"

This really is like Alice 'reaching out' to her for the first time. An overture of friendship.

"I don't know, Alice. I haven't got any grass in Hythe, just a patio. I think I would go with Astroturf?"

I'm expecting a sneer, but Alice looks intrigued.

"No mowing?"

"Well, no, it's fake grass," replies Linda a little drily. "Very realistic, I believe."

"What about the dogs' you-know-what?"

"Ah, well, you know, it can just be hosed down. Bob's your uncle."

They're getting on like a house on fire! Alice goes and sits closer to Linda, no doubt hoping for other cut-price tips and suggestions.

Denis clears his throat loudly: "Look, this is all well and good, but we drove up here for a reason, Linda, and it seems nothing's been sorted."

Linda and Alice lookup as one; they were irritated that their bonding session was interrupted before it even started.

"There's really nothing we can do, is there?" says Linda. "My review—I can't delete it now—was pretty effective as revenge for not getting a full refund—"

"I'll say!" cries Alice. "I might as well give up trying to run an Airbnb. But then I guess Louise's mouse-droppings review has had pretty much the same effect? Not that it was anything to do with me. Sheer coincidence."

"Oh, come on, pull the other one!" Louise snorts. "It's too late for that now. Look, guys, the whole point is, don't you realise those Airbnb guys in San Francisco are literally unable to cancel those reviews—there's no mechanism in place to do it, that's just how it's set up."

"As I said," resumes Denis. "It really would have been much better for all concerned if you, Alice, had just taken the hit from Linda—"

Linda groans, and Alice looks up to the heavens. They really are singing from the same hymn sheet now.

"Not going to happen," I say for the second time.

"Well, but now look at the pair of you," says Denis. "Coming from the pugilistic community as I do, I've witnessed a cockfight in my time, and it's a pathetic sight, I can tell you. You just end up with these two bloody, broken-winged creatures, and all for what?"

"Steady on!" Alice interrupts.

"Yes, well, pardon my metaphor, but you're both, like, well, done for, really?"

"Oh, but are we?" Linda looks like she's hatching some sort of idea. She actually grabs Alice's hand.

"Look, now life's misfortunes have pushed us together, how about this for an idea. We bypass the big boys, the so-called 'Airbnb Community' and all that, and join forces in a little independent venture!"

"Seaside and City!" Louise offers, one step ahead as usual.

"Well, yes!"

"Competing Cacophonies: Trains and Seagulls!" I contribute but just get a few annoyed looks.

"I'm in!" Alice decides. "Isn't this exciting?" She almost seems to be welling up.

"You'll have to try and get a little closer to my level when it comes to standards," remarks Linda then.

Uh-oh.

Alice is bristling. "What do you mean?"

"Well, I mean, you've only got to look under the dogs' chair. There in the corner."

All three dogs are sitting on Alice's old Lloyd Loom armchair, staring back at her as if to say, "It wasn't me!"

The floor under the chair has got a thick coating of grey dust. Oh, dear. "Oh, no! That's just because the Common's so muddy right now. It dries on their fur, and then it sort of gets sieved through the open weave of the chair. You haven't got dogs, so you wouldn't know."

"Well, here's an idea, we'll get some of those Dyson Animal vacuums!" says Linda, having a good slug of wine. Panic over. "Oh, and I know what I wanted to ask you—are the trains on strike?"

"No way," says Alice. "Why?"

"I can't hear any."

"Well, that's what I tried to explain to you—it's literally only about four hours out of twenty-four."

"To be fair, they make the most of those four hours!" Linda counters. "But look, I've got a confession to make to you: I've always had a phobia of trains ever since I was very young—six years old—"

"But didn't you read the blurb in the listing?" says Alice.

"No, no, I didn't, I just thought, as you were Super Host status—"

"Not even sure how that happened," murmurs Louise.

"How did this phobia develop?" asks Araminta hastily.

"Well, you know the Dymchurch and Hythe Light Railway?"

"Yes, I know it well!"

"I fell off!"

"Fell off?" asks more than one person.

"Well," says Araminta knowledgeably, "it's like a children's train with dinky painted wooden carriages, but it's a proper steam train, goes all the way to Dungeness!"

"Oh," says Louise wistfully, "if only we'd known, we could have gone on it!"

"Well, you still can, now!" says Linda. "Except I won't come with you."

"You poor thing!" says Alice. And they hug again!

"I hate to spoil the vibe," says Louise, "but it is now actually 2am. I'm guessing it's going to be a mass sleepover?"

"You can sleep in my spare room, Denis." I offer. "Come on, Louise, let's get some sheets and stuff."

"OK, Araminta, Linda and me down here!" says Alice jovially. "The Airbnb's empty, as we know…this is fun! And a full English breakfast for all of us in the morning to celebrate!"

"Make that some pieces of burnt toast," I mutter as we exit.

"If they're lucky," says Louise.

Alice aged seven

The End

CPSIA information can be obtained
at www.ICGtesting.com
Printed in the USA
LVHW040939290322
714698LV00015B/753

9 781398 414617